I Don't Want to Be Like You

By Maryanne Christiano-Mistretta

Copyright © 2018 by Maryanne Christiano-Mistretta (Higher Ground Books & Media)
All rights reserved. No part of this publication may be reproduced may be reproduced in any form, stored in a retrieval system, or transmitted in any form, or by any means (electronic, mechanical, photocopying, recording or otherwise) without prior permission by the copyright owner and the publisher of this book.

All scripture quotations unless otherwise noted are taken from the New Revised Standard Version (NRSV) of the Bible, copyright ® 1989 by the Division of Christian Education of the National Council of the Churches of Christ in the United States of America, and are used by permission. All rights reserved.
The scripture quotation noted KJV is from the King James Version of the Holy Bible commissioned in 1604 by King James I of England and completed in 1611. The KJV is public domain in the United States.
The scripture quotation noted CEV is taken from the Holy Bible Contemporary English Version, copyright ® 1995 by the American Bible Society, also used by permission. All rights reserved.

Higher Ground Books & Media
Springfield, Ohio.
http://highergroundbooksandmedia.com

Printed in the United States of America 2018

I Don't Want to Be Like You

By Maryanne Christiano-Mistretta

Emma!
Super meeting you!
Keep rockin' it.
LOVE
Maryanne xxoo

DEDICATION

Dedicated to anyone who dares to be YOUnique!

Foreword

"It's better to walk a lonely path than be in the company of a fool."
-- Buddha.

Does this explain why so many fools belong to cliques? Possibly. It takes a strong person to break away from the herd. It takes a strong person to be his/herself, to stand up for his/herself, and risk ridicule and scorn. The thing is, when a person is fierce enough to do that, the act only makes the person greater.

"Only the strong survive" is an intense, honest statement. It takes a long time to become strong and the strong usually learn at a very young age. As young as 13, I realized the foolishness of herd mentality and was overwhelmed by my young intelligence. I often cried because I felt ahead of my time. My mother comforted me by saying, "You're a leader, not a follower."

I worked hard all my life to stand up for what I believe in. I once stood up to a publisher who didn't treat me with respect. I got hired at a better publishing company three days later; for better pay. I let go of boyfriends who didn't allow me to grow to my full potential. I've ended friendships because of girls who were catty. It's important to let go of anything that holds you back.
Happiness can be work. Studying the works of G. I. Gurdjieff wasn't an easy task at age 24 and it wouldn't be any easier if I started studying Gurdjieff now. But once the vehicles are etched in your brain, it's as if it's etched in rock. The work turns into a precious gift. That gift can never be taken from you because you worked so hard for it.

The sad part is, people become jealous of this gift and want to oppress you. Happiness and confidence is a threat to some people. What they don't realize is that they, too, can have this gift.
But to them, it's easier to criticize, toss stones, and be jealous than to work on their own beings. They prefer to hide inside a box; being with a clique of others who don't think for themselves. Because they are afraid to ask questions. Because they are afraid to stand up for themselves. Because being happy means breaking away from herd mentality.

We are all created as perfect human beings. Our potential extends many galaxies and universes. Why do people refuse to believe this and not accept the gift?
If you are part of a herd, you will never be truly happy. You have to

think out of the box.

The most empowering thing about being a bully survivor is overcoming the shame. When you're a child or a teen being picked on, you believe it's your fault, that you deserve it. You may even think you are all the bad things the bullies call you. And that is furthest from the truth.

In my research about bullying, it's more about the bully than the child being picked on. The bully is the one with the issues; the one who was hurt at home, or even jealous of his/her victim. Yes, jealous. If you do a Google search on celebrities who were bullied, you certainly won't come up empty handled. People who were bullied had a little something extra special that others didn't. They were different. They were YOUnique. And they ended up successful in life.

But that doesn't make the hurt any less. Being afraid to go to school is tragic. No child should feel that way. It's not fair and it's detrimental to one's studies.

When I was bullied, throughout grade school and high school, it was the most sickening thing you can imagine because it was constant. Yet, unlike many young people today, it never occurred to me to end my life. My dreams were always, "When I get out of school…" I just knew in my heart there was bigger world.

But the hurt was so embedded in my brain, when I had my first job at 18, I was thrilled that no one called me a "scumbag." Little did I realize that jealous adults acted differently than jealous children and teenagers. They do things passive-aggressively. But that is much easier to deal with. You can ignore so much in the adult world because you make it your own. As a child, you just don't have that kind of power yet.

What makes a person a target for bullying? In many cases, it *is* jealousy. But also, in some cases, it could unintentionally be the target's fault, which is why a student can go from one school to another and still be bullied. For example, a child from a divorced home reeks of insecurity. Other kids feel the vibes of someone who doesn't have confidence and use it to their advantage. Nevertheless, it's still no excuse for bullying. Schools are finally realizing this and teaching tools to parents, so they can support their child.

My heart goes out to anyone reading this who has been bullied as a child or teen. Or is reading this as a child or teen and being bullied. If I can prevent just one child or teen from committing suicide, then my work is done. I want to say to every child or teen that you are special and have something great to offer to the world. Don't let anyone take that away from you. And you must believe, it does get better!

I worked very hard to get over the hurt and shame. When I read my diaries in order to write this book, I thought a few things about the bullies. *Were they bullied at home? What about themselves made them so insecure they had to pick on me and others to feel better about themselves?* And, finally, *I hope they changed. I wish them well and that they are raising good children, not bullies.*

If I were to meet any of my "bullies" today, I'd probably thank them for making me such a strong person. However, some children don't get out of it alive. There are so many suicides that were the devastating result of bullying. I want kids to KNOW that life isn't always this way.

May my path inspire you to make your own beautiful way in this world. You are a special being and there's a big world out there waiting for you to make a difference!

Chapter 1

The very first time I was bullied, it wasn't personal. I was about 9-years-old and living in West Paterson, New Jersey with my parents and my little sister, Kim. My grandparents lived in the house next door. It was in the 1970s and a different time. There was no such thing as online bullying yet. Some bullies were exactly like you saw on old television shows. Those were the bullies that weren't so hurtful. Hear me out…

Kim and I liked to take walks around the block. About midway around the block, there was this old, shabby house. In that house lived about four kids, two boys, and two girls. All cute and blue-eyed with dirty blonde hair. But they always looked a mess. Their hair was knotted. They wore ragged clothes. If you ever watched "Little House on the Prairie" they would remind you of the bad kids on that show. Seeing them was like going back in time.

The first time we passed their house, all four yelled at us in unison, "Get off our property!" We weren't on their property, just the sidewalk in front of their house. We kept walking. And they chased us. The girl that was about my age grabbed me by the hair and started beating me. My sister was about 6 and there was a younger girl in that family that was hitting her too. We escaped, but that didn't stop us from taking a walk around the block. We were more careful the next time. When we passed the house, we'd cross the street and walk very fast.

This type of bullying didn't bother me. Taking those walks around the block was fun and scary, like going into a spook house. You see, getting hit is frightening to a child, but it's nothing compared to verbal abuse. When someone calls you things like "dog" "scumbag" "space cadet" or "whore" it hurts your heart deeply. When someone threatens you and says they are going to "beat the shit out of you" or "ruin your pretty face" and you're the smallest and skinniest kid in the classroom, it's more terrifying than if they just did it. Because you're always in a state of anticipating the worst. No kid should live like that. But I did way back when and many still do today.

My parents divorced when I was in third grade. That's the time my grades dropped too. I never liked my father, but I can't remember why. Or maybe I blocked the reason out of my head. After my parents divorced he had visitation rights. Then the day came when my mother said, "Daddy isn't going to come here anymore." I was secretly glad.

Years later I wanted to know him. I did things that put me in the public eye. Before I became a writer, I did some modeling. My photos were in newspapers; and even an ice skating catalog. I prayed that maybe my father would see the photos and look me up. That never happened. This was all before the internet, so I had no idea how to try to find him. And it never occurred to me to go to a detective.

When I asked my mother about him, she wouldn't have much to say. So, I let it go.

First and second grade I was a straight-A student. My first-grade teacher was a friend of my grandmother's. She was beautiful, looking like Marlo Thomas of "That Girl." And she was incredibly sweet. She wore miniskirts and white go-go boots. And I was teacher's pet. I was cute, quiet, and read faster than any other student. I kept requesting more school books to read. The teacher was proud of me.

My second-grade teacher was cool too. She played guitar and was also very pretty. One day in the playground a girl in my class lifted my skirt up. I did the same right back to her, but I was the one who got caught. The teacher hollered at me. I was so upset I told my mother when I went home for lunch. My mother drove me back to school and reprimanded the teacher. The teacher apologized for yelling at me and was super nice to me afterwards, offering me a bite of her sandwich.

By third grade, around the time of the divorce, I was doing terrible in school. When you got a bad grade in school, your parents had to sign the paper. I never had my mother sign them. I hid the papers that were marked D and F. Then for whatever reason, I decided to come clean. I showed my grandmother first.

"Don't show your mother," she said and encouraged me to "get rid of them."

Then it became mandatory for a parent to sign a bad paper. I tried to get around it by asking my mother for her autograph, then taping it on to the paper myself. It looked bad. Finally, I showed her the paper.

"Is that all you're worried about?" my mother asked. She was in a good mood and signed the school paper. After that day I tried hard and started getting good grades again.

Throughout third and fourth grades I had a normal, happy childhood. Then we moved.

Chapter 2

To this day I love the smell of fresh paint. My grandfather brought a gorgeous house in Cedar Grove, New Jersey, and we moved the summer before I started fifth grade. The house was big enough to comfortably fit my grandparents, my mother, me, my sister, and even my great grandmother.

I anticipated a happy life on Marley Avenue. We had a huge backyard with a garden and a pool. Up the street was a Chinese restaurant. The fortune cookies were freshly baked; so soft you could open them up with ease and get your fortune. Next to the Chinese restaurant was a convenience store that had candy, so we called it "The Candy Store." We could walk to the candy store from our home. We lived on a dead-end street, so we could ride our bikes, walk our pocket-sized poodles, and play ball in the street without worrying too much about cars.

There were many kids on that block and we had much fun over the years. My family was always generous, letting our friends come over to swim in the pool. We always had cookies and treats in the house. And if someone wanted to stay for dinner, there was plenty.

In our neighborhood, there was a girl who was rather big for her age and the oldest kid on the block, at least a year older than me. In the beginning, I looked up to her. She was an incredible artist. She came to America from Germany. I'll call her Brit.

While I looked up to Brit, it seemed to me that she idolized my mother. She always said, "Your mother is so pretty" and would look at her starry eyed. Sometimes I think she was my friend just to be close to my mother. If you do a Google search on the entertainer from the 1960s, Joey Heatherton, that's who my mom looked like when she was a young mother. Same haircut and all. The original "hot mom."

One day, Brit and I were hanging out in the swimming pool with my younger sister, cousin, and some other kids. Brit started rough necking with the other kids and accidentally splashed my mother who was on the deck. My mother yelled at her because she just had her hair done.

Brit got quiet. Then from that day on she didn't want to be my friend anymore. I didn't put two and two together back then; I was just a kid. But in later years I figured it out. She was a kid herself, embarrassed about my mom reprimanding her. I commend Brit for having respect for my mom and not sassing her; however, this is where my problems began. Brit started taking her anger, towards my mother, out on me.

When I started school that September, I was the new kid. I was enthusiastic about that. It meant a fresh start. My mother dressed my sister and I beautifully. At the start of the school year we'd shop in Macy's and she'd get us great outfits.

In this suburban public school, kids were a little too low key. They went to school in jeans looking sloppy. So, I stood out with my nice clothes. I was also very quiet.

To be honest, I was never one to want to fit in with other kids. At home I was always around adults and their lives seemed so much fun. My mother was young, beautiful, and divorced. She hung out with my cool uncle who was also divorced. Then there was my grandmother. She worked as a short order cook in a tavern owned by my step-grandfather's son. I always eavesdropped to hear my mother, uncle, and grandmother speak about the crazy fun times at that bar, The Black Forest Inn.

On Friday and Saturday nights I'd get to go to the tavern and help my grandmother in the kitchen. I'd help her fill coleslaw cups and wash dishes. Then she'd give money for comic books.

In the tavern was a jukebox with all the great Top 40 hits of the early 1970s. But the highlight of the night was when the jukebox got turned off, and an amazing live band called Donna Lori and the Music Box played.

Donna Lori was stunning. She had the long, straight black Cher-hair thing going on. And she really liked me. She invited me to sing onstage with her. I was only 10 and didn't know how to sing, but the adults in the bar thought it was cute.

She also had a daughter she'd bring to the bar with her who was around my age. We got along great. So why was I having a problem making friends at school? I can only put bits and pieces together to try to figure it out. Since I'm not a bully myself, I don't know how the mind of a bully works. Even though I didn't want to be like anyone else, I didn't want them to harass me either. I just wanted to be left alone, to read, do my work, and then come home and play.

"Say 'a word'" is something I often heard from school boys. That didn't bother me. I just didn't answer them.

One day we were going on a class trip and everyone has a

partner to sit with on the bus. I didn't. The teacher insisted I pick a partner.

Put on the spot, I chose a girl I thought was nice. However, she was mad at me for picking her because she had another friend she wanted to sit with. This is when the harassment officially started. All the girls ganged up on me and kept saying mean things to me throughout the ride there and back. It made the class trip miserable for me. I cried.

Then one girl, I'll call Jean, told me not to get upset and explained that they already picked their bus partners. Back then, girls didn't hug each other like they do today. I think if we hugged, that would have created a bond and maybe it would have brought me out of my shell. However, I continued to be quiet.

A few months later Jean wanted me to come to her house for a "makeover." She wanted to see what I'd look like in blue jeans. I went along with it. The idea was also for me to get a boyfriend--at 10-years-old.

Kids in my school smoked and bragged about things they did with boys. They named sexual acts by bases: Base 1, Base 2, Base 3. No one ever said they went "all the way" though.

The idea of having a boyfriend mortified me. This is another reason I didn't fit in. And when I finally did kiss a boy for the first time, I was only 13. Way too young. I guess that's how it was in the suburbs in the 1970s.

My friends today who have children well into their teen years have not yet had their first kiss or first boyfriend. That to me is a better pace. I regret that I gave in to peer pressure back then. I feel a bit of my childhood was robbed.

Anyway, I liked the jeans and begged my mother and grandmother to take me shopping so I can fit in. They did. But it was the wrong brand. This is when the harassment started, mainly from Jean and Brit, making fun of my jeans.

I remember was coming home crying. My grandmother said, "What are you crying about them for? They ain't worth your spit."

In addition to the verbal harassment from Jean and Brit there were bullies who liked to fight physically. My grandmother had advice about this too, "Just give them one good punch to show them you're not afraid of them."

One day a bully came charging at me like a bull while I was going home for lunch. I was carrying my science book to study during my lunch break. She started getting closer. Her face was red, and she looked like a devil. My adrenaline kicked in and I hit her hard over the head with my science book. I hurt her, and she backed off. She never bothered me again. If only I could use my mouth the way I used my hands that day and give all the verbal abusive bullies a piece of my mind. But at school I was in a clam shell. I just couldn't do it. And anyone who is introverted knows exactly what that's like. You just can't explain it to an outgoing person. Nowadays I'm extremely outgoing. Would you believe public speaking is one of the ways I earn a living?

Mind you, I did have my moments. For instance, I was very good at roller skating and won third place in a roller skating limbo contest that was held in the school gym on Saturdays. I also made up a dance to the song "Venus," the Tom Jones version, which I performed on talent day. I was certainly not shy when it came to creativity and being in the limelight. One day in art class the assignment was to take a magazine picture, rip it in half, and draw the other half. I choose a tiger-striped cat. My drawing was one of the best, so they hung it up in the hallway for everyone to see.

I remember praise from teachers, but never from fellow students. And even though I was naturally athletic, because we had a big yard and a swimming pool, I was always chosen last for the teams in gym. This discouraged me from wanting to exercise in school. And eventually I stopped exercising at home too. I remember walking up a hill when I was 15 huffing and puffing.

Then there was the day I overheard a bunch of girls badmouthing me. Jean was telling everyone that her mother said that I was so pretty I was going to be the most popular kid in high school. Again, it was a kid taking it out on me because of what seemed like rejection from an adult. It wasn't my fault her mom said that, but it provoked Jean to be even nastier to me, with Brit chiming in. The two were always the ring leaders.

Jean was Jewish, and I mentioned before that Brit was German. They always made fun of me for being Italian. They told jokes with Italian slurs and laughed at me. Kids often repeat derogatory comments they may have heard at home from their prejudiced parents. I pity their parents for raising their children this way.

So, what were my sins to deserve this constant harassment? I honestly couldn't figure it out. I was so quiet I never said anything nasty to anyone. Okay, so they didn't like the nice clothes my mother got for me at Macy's and my jeans weren't the right brand. I was different and quiet, but I still wanted to be friends with people. I didn't have a bad bone in my body. They didn't have to like me or be friends with me. But they didn't have to stalk and hassle me either.

Then they started getting on my case about my mother, who dressed sexy. I had to hear that she was coming to school with her "tits hanging out." And that she was "flirting" with male teachers. Their spiteful words were always loud enough for me to hear. It was all exaggerations that came from a catty place. But again, was it coming from directly from the young girls? Or their parents? Could their moms be jealous of my mom? Hmm…

My mother went to the school to address my troubles. She even went to Brit's home and spoke to her dad. She got nowhere.

His mindset was, "Not my little darling."

The bullying in school continued to be relentless and eventually my mother thought it would be best to take me out of the public school and put me in a Catholic school. I was now 12 and in the middle of 7th grade.

I DON'T WANT TO BE LIKE YOU

Chapter 3

The first few months of Catholic school were nice. I was still quiet but expressed myself artistically as usual. Even though I enrolled in the middle of the year, I got to be in the Christmas play. It was "Happy Days," based on the famous television show in the 1970s. My mother put my hair up in a high ponytail and I got to wear blue eyeshadow, which was popular during that time. One of the boys in the eighth-grade said I was "cute." My role was small. I was cast as Potsie's girlfriend.

It wasn't long after I started Catholic school that I realized these kids weren't much better than the kids at the public school. On my very first day I heard the gossip. One of the girls told me to stay away from another girl who had a bad reputation. She was always picked on. And secretly, as well as shamefully, I was relieved it wasn't me being singled out. I never joined in though. Bullying just wasn't my style. The girl with the "bad reputation" once smiled at me. I was too shy to smile back, but I did invite her to a party I had the following year.

I made friends with another girl who seemed to be a loner. She was pretty, tall, and very thin. I'll call her Lacey.

We'd go over each other houses. We'd also talk on the phone for hours. Eventually we both ended up getting bullied at the Catholic school. We reconnected in later years thanks to Face Book and had lunch. In her late 40s, she looked like a model. And during our conversation, she said the truest thing about the bullies, "What did *they* have to offer?" She was right!

I can't speak for Lacey, but during this time I felt the worst and ugliest I felt in my entire life. First off, I ended up needing glasses. Back then glasses weren't fashionable like they are today. But I was proud to get them because my mother wore them; and my cool uncle wore them too. I got two pair; one regular, and one tinted for outdoors.

Wearing them to school I got called the typical names like "four-eyes." But it got worse, I was called "dog" and "scumbag" too. Both boys and girls would bark at me when I walked past them in the halls.

When I started wearing glasses, I also started carrying a handbag so I could put my glasses away when I went to gym. In my bag, I carried other girl type items like lip gloss and a carry case for my mini and maxi pads.

Somehow, someone, without my knowledge, went through my purse and stole my maxi pad case. Then one of the boys saw me and threw the pads at me. But my case wasn't with them. I was so upset that I didn't have the case, I had to wrap them up in tissues to transport them with me. The case came with a "starter kit" that girls purchased in school when we first learned about menstruation. I was so proud of that kit. Every day I'd check my underwear, hoping to get my period because it meant I was "all grown up."

What was my hurry? I didn't enjoy being a kid anymore.

So, as silly as it may sound, I was devastated that I lost the case. But to make matters worse, the bullies in the school made sure this incident made it to the school newspaper. The Catholic school teachers did nothing about it.

Aside from Lacey, I made another friend. I'll call her Sally. She was pretty and always wore these cool bright green Converse sneakers. Unexpectedly, Sally called me at home and asked me if I wanted to go swimming with her on a Friday night. A local college had indoor swimming. It was enticing because I loved swimming and since it was winter, our pool had the cover on it for several months.

My gut told me "no" and in my heart, I would rather stay home and hang out with my grandmother. As they say nowadays, I was "not feeling it."

I went anyway. We had a nice time and started to get close. Just like with Lacey, I'd talk on the phone with Sally for hours and we'd go over each other houses. The difference was, Sally had a mean streak. She seemed to have a strong craving, one I never understood, to be like the "popular" girls. And she used me as a scapegoat to take out whatever hostility she had towards the popular girls.

On the surface she was very nice, so her bad behavior was deceiving. We had plenty of fun times and laughter together. I still crack up over some of the fun we once had.

But then the little digs started. I was a thin, tiny girl, but now developing breasts and an ass. Sally was tall and husky. She seemed to resent that I was small, and she would focus on my flaws--according to her. She told me: I couldn't sing, I talked to her about music too much, and I needed to get out of my shell. The fact that I opened-up to her wasn't good enough. She was one year older, in eighth grade, and often bossed me around. My uncle didn't like her and made sure I knew it.

Sally told me one of her father's friends said I was "built like a brick shit house." Looking back, it was a creepy thing for a grown man to say about a girl who was only 13. But I took it as a big compliment and enjoyed the attention from a grown up.

Around this time, I started to love the music of Queen. "A Night at the Opera" was out for some time and they had just released the single "Somebody to Love" from their sixth album "A Day at the Races." I got all the albums from a record store, but it was very hard finding their second album, "Queen II."

Back then you didn't have the instant satisfaction you have today--ordering something online and getting it within 48 hours. No, you had to wait. I didn't even know if record stores could order something for you. We were a very different generation of kids. If you didn't have something you wanted, you could wait a very long time for it.

With my love for Queen, it was lead singer Freddie Mercury I wanted to be like, not the kids at school. I went to school with black nail polish painted on my left hand, as Freddie Mercury did. I practiced his moves in the mirror and to this day I can imitate his moves flawlessly.

I developed a nail polish fixation and besides painting black on my left hand, I'd paint my nails a different color every day. The boys in school noticed, but that wasn't a good thing.

"What color is it today, Christiano?" one of the boys asked me in disgust. That particular boy was the same one who asked me out in later years when we'd see each other in a NJ gothic/alternative music club called The Loop Lounge, in Passaic, New Jersey. We were now in our early 30s and he said to me, "You wore glasses, but you were always cute." I took this as his way of apologizing to me. He was sincere. For the record, I didn't date him. I was never interested in him that way, but I'm glad he made peace with me.

Perhaps my grandmother was right, "They pick on you because they like you." But "dog" and "scumbag" are very harsh words. I would have settled for "four-eyes."

Negative words coming at you from all directions--boys and girls, in both seventh and eighth grades--is horrible. Even if you like being unique that's no reason for being verbally tortured day in and day out. I started skipping classes. I'll never forget a nun trying to find me as I went from hallway to stairwell to continue hiding.

When I came home, I lost all interest in going outdoors. Instead I'd do my homework and close the door of my room. I'd listen to all five Queen albums; in the order they were released. This was my routine every day. I had now found Queen II. It was one of the most exciting days in my life seeing it in the Queen bin in Korvettes, a popular discount store founded in the 1940s, ceasing operation in 1980. There were other discount stores Two Guys and Great Eastern. My grandmother would take me and my little sister. I'd always hit the record sections. One day we passed a camera section and a sales man took a Polaroid picture of us. If this happened today, the man would be labeled a creep. But, again, I enjoyed the attention. He was very nice to us and we always stopped by to say "Hi" to him.

I always got along great with older people. They were fascinating, and I held much respect. Even when I first started working, I'd rather hang out with women 20 to 50 years older than me instead of those in my peer group who bored me with senseless gossip and their keeping up with the Joneses mentality.

When I listened to my Queen records, I went into a zone where I'd imagine my life as an adult. The first thing on my list was getting contact lenses. I'd practice my smile in the mirror and tell myself I'd be so pretty when I got rid of the glasses.

In addition to being called "dog" and "scumbag" the next thing I was known as was a "stiff" which traditionally means a dead body. I earned that title for not having a boyfriend.

People today will be astonished when they read this because as I wrote earlier, back in the 1970s, kids started young.

Interesting, I somehow got the two best looking boys in the eighth grade interested in me. They came over, at separate times of course, and would put their arms around me. It felt good for a very long time. Then they'd go in for a kiss and I just couldn't do it. I would say, "Not yet." Their frustration was obvious, and they'd go home soon afterwards.

I guess boys will be boys and word got out that nothing happened, and I paid for it with the title "stiff." Then the anonymous phone calls started. But I gotta admit, when Sally was over my house and these calls would come in, we'd have a blast joking around with the callers. One time she convinced me to call a guy *she* liked and tell him I wanted to have sex with him. Like an idiot, I listened.

I guess he recognized our voices and approached us

immediately the next day. He looked our way but couldn't really look us in the eye. Teenage awkwardness on his end. He was cute, but chubby. Not someone the girls went crazy for. He mumbled, "What prick called me up?"

Sally and I looked at each other and laughed. Then she said, "Did you hear what he said?"

I said, "No." I really didn't.

She repeated, "What prick called me up?"

I never heard of a girl being called a "prick" before. But young people back then weren't as smart and sophisticated as they are today. At least not in the suburbs of New Jersey.

Then after that, word got out, and everyone started calling me a whore. Sally gave me the attitude that I deserved it, even though she was the one who coaxed me to call him.

I asked, "Isn't it better than being called a stiff?"

She said, "No." And it didn't stop her from manipulating me even further.

Of course, everyone has a mind of their own. But at this point, I'd do anything to keep a friend, even if the friend wasn't such a good one.

Sally had a friend I'll call Aaron. He wasn't that cute, but I wanted to kiss a boy because all the other girls were doing it. I told her I liked him, and she was quick to set something up. My first kiss was awful. My lips burned for a long time afterward. I knew deep down I wasn't interested in him, so I just said, "Thank you for being Freddie Mercury."

And, respectively, he said, "Thank you for being Stevie Nicks."

So that was that.

No matter what, I continued to get verbally bullied in seventh grade. One day I was in the bathroom and an eighth-grade girl, I'll call Edith, pushed me against the wall and grabbed my hands so that I couldn't move. Her entire body was against me, as she held my hands, in front of my stomach. I was terrified.

She looked me straight in the eye, with a growl on her face, and said, "What are you gonna do now, scum?"

With that, I stuck my thumb into her stomach as hard as I could. She backed off and screamed some obscenities at me.

Turned out, she wasn't too popular with other eighth grade girls. They really disliked her for some reason. Suddenly, I was a hero.

One of the eighth graders said to me, "Nice fight with Edith!"

She had a huge smile on her face.

Her friends approached me, one by one, and said, "Yeah, nice fight!"

From then on, the eighth-grade girls were nice to me. And so were the eighth-grade boys. Yet, I still heard "dog" and "scumbag" every day from the seventh graders.

When I shared my concern with Sally, she said, "Well, who would you rather be friends with, the seventh graders or the eighth graders?"

The eighth graders. It made sense.

So, a few weeks before school let out for summer, I decided to have a party. And I only invited the eighth graders. Word got out, and seventh graders started being nice to me and begging me to go to the party.

At our house in Cedar Grove, we had a basement, that was not quite furnished, but nice enough to hold a party. I invited all the seventh and eighth graders. Kiss's album "Destroyer" was recently released and I played the same record over and over all night as my classmates came with alcoholic beverages. Soon kids were getting drunk. One girl was in a heavy make-out session with a boy. There were two stand-out moments of the evening. One was when a cute boy sang "Beth" to me but changed the words to "Maryanne."

Another stand out was when one of the most popular girls from seventh grade got drunk. She was crying, but still wanted more to drink when the well ran dry at the party. "I want to go to a liquor store!" she shouted over and over.

I tried to comfort her by going over to her. I didn't do anything because I was still shy. I just sat next to her. She saw me and screamed at me. "I want to be with my friends!"

I knew at that moment I was just being used for the party. I was not a "friend." Afterwards, back in school, I got the cold shoulder treatment from both grades. And I got in trouble for having alcohol at the party. I was honest with my mother and told her I was drinking, even though I only had a swig or two of beer. I thought she'd appreciate my honesty, instead she yelled, "What's next?! Drugs?!"

It was not fun being me at that point. Summer came and went, and I don't really remember much of eighth grade, except the summer after I graduated.

I begged my mother to let me go to Neuman Prep, an expensive private high school in Wayne, New Jersey. I wanted to go there because that's where Sally went. She constantly raved about the school and how nice everyone was. Sally finally got what she always wanted—popularity.

My mother said, "yes" and I looked forward to high school.

Chapter 4

That summer, I was about to turn 14 and finally became interested in boys. I was lucky, my first boyfriend was like gold in many ways. I'll call him Brian and he was 19; a five-and-a-half-year age difference. My family disapproved. But I was stubborn and snuck out to see him.

Brian treated me like royalty. There was no rush for sex, but it was the first kiss I really liked. He took me everywhere: concerts, movies, dinners. And he showered me with gifts like records and flowers. One time we had a fight and Meat Loaf, a 1970s rock star, was at a local mall signing autographs. Brian went as far as standing in line to meet Meat Loaf, having him write me a note, so I'd forgive him.

Entering my freshman-year at high school with a boyfriend gave me a confidence I never had before. Even Sally noticed. But she was quick to point out that it seemed Brian was the only one I trusted.

It was true. Sally and I drifted apart. She barely acknowledged me at Neumann Prep, and she was the reason I wanted to go there! But she was right about the kids there being so nice.

On the school bus there were two extraordinary beautiful girls. They looked like models. They talked bad ass and smoked. I wanted to be cool too. I wasn't interested in smoking, so I started a rumor that I was pregnant. Word got out and it seemed so shocking to some, so I back tracked and made sure people knew that wasn't true. And all was forgiven. The students in this school were classier than those I knew in my past. I was in awe of so many of them. For once, it was okay to just be myself. No one at Neumann Prep ever made fun of me. Not even when I got my hair feathered and had a hard time styling it. I went to school looking stupid until it grew back all one length again. From freshman to seniors, they were all good kids. Never had a problem there. Sure, there were cliques, but if you weren't in the clique, it was just fine. Those students would still say "hello" to you or smile at you. Even the bad ass girls. And there was a guy who liked Queen that I could talk to as well.

I brought Brian with me to a Battle of the Bands and everyone liked him. Girls asked me all the time, "How is Brian?" They were so nice, sweet, and cute. I wish I kept in touch with them or remembered their names. I was still in my shy stage. Plus, you had to keep your grades high to stay in the school. I was always tired from studying and sneaking out to see Brian.

My mother was wise to this and tried to use reverse psychology on me. She did not want me getting serious at such a young age. And I kind of agreed. Brian insisted he loved me, but what did I know about love at age 14? I'd see girls crying in school because their boyfriends broke up with them. I never had that experience of hurt before. I wanted to hang out with girlfriends and do things with people besides Brian. I was also starting to get a little boy crazy, checking out guys my own age. There was one who looked like Barry Williams, aka Greg Brady from "The Brady Bunch." He put his arm around me on the bus after a school trip. I felt guilty for talking to him and liking him because I was committed.

Soon after that, I broke up with Brian. To this day I feel bad for hurting him. And for anyone I've ever hurt. But from being bullied so much, I lost a great sense of trust for people. I never learned how to make a true friend until my later years. I was with Brian for eight months, which seemed like a lifetime. I was confused after we broke up and didn't rush into another relationship. In fact, I didn't date anyone for months.

My mother decided not to enroll me in Neumann Prep for another year. Her reasoning was that all I ever did was study and I was tired all the time because I got up at 5 a.m. to get ready and then catch the bus. Plus, "You don't want to go to college anyway," she said.

Back then, kids weren't given a choice like they are today. It was always the mother's decision. And she sounded so convincing, that sleeping later in the morning would be a great reason to leave Neumann Prep.

And as a freshman I wasn't even thinking about college, so I just said, "Okay." Then, BAM--Straight to the public school. Straight to hell.

Chapter 5

The summer of 1977. I was 14, going on 15, about to enter sophomore year. My mother was remarried and lived with my stepfather. My sister and I went back and forth to live with her; or my grandmother, grandfather, and great grandmother in the big house in Cedar Grove.

We lived about 10 minutes away from a local shopping mall. Most of the summer, my sister and I hung out at the mall where we met two nice girls we got along with. One of them was obese, and super funny; the other was thin as a toothpick. The obese one referred to herself as "The Fox." She was able to laugh at herself, which was great. All summer long the four of us hung out together, checking out boys. If a really cute boy would walk by, The Fox say, "My Christmas present!" and she would start following him, but then turn around and come back. We'd all have a great laugh. She was a hoot.

I now evolved from ugly duckling to swan! My auburn hair was super long. I was thin. And I was no longer hiding behind glasses, I had contact lenses. Life was getting fun.

Near the end of the summer, my mother decided to take the family on a vacation to Wildwood, a seashore resort in New Jersey. Wildwood was over three hours from our home. Mom asked me if I'd like to take The Fox with us. I really didn't want to. Again, it was a gut feeling like I had with Sally. But since my mother asked, I trusted it was a good idea and said "yes."

We ended up having an amazing vacation, except for one night. We were walking the boardwalk, something got in my eye and I wanted to go back to the hotel to take out my contact lens and flush my eyes. My mother was frustrated because we had to go back to the hotel. She told me to take my contacts out and not wear them for the rest of the trip.

I still had glasses, but they were only used around the house. I thought if I put my glasses on, I'd transport back to dog land and that kids on the boardwalk would make fun of me. This is how bullying has such a negative effect on young people. It traumatizes you and makes you incredibly insecure. Even with all my positive experiences at Neumann Prep, and the positive experience of dating Brian (who actually liked me in my glasses!) the trauma from grade school was still embedded in my psyche. Sometimes, bad things take a long time to get over.

So, the rest of the trip, I walked around half blind. My eyesight was terrible. (And it still is, but I must say according to my eye doctor, I am only very nearsighted. I have a very healthy retina and my eyes in general are in good health with no damage).

This all sounds terribly vain. And it also sounds so bad because I was only 15. One may think I was a "spoiled brat." But hear me out. If you've never been bullied I will try to explain to you. There must be something you are insecure about, everyone is. Suppose you have something you feel makes your style POP and it was suddenly taken away from you. Maybe a signature hairstyle or color? Maybe your favorite pair of boots or your skinny jeans? Maybe if you were told you had to take out your nose ring or laser away your favorite tattoo?

So, I was upset and crying because A. my mother was mad at me; and B. I couldn't see unless I wore my hideous glasses.

The Fox comforted me a with great big hug. I never had that kind of love from a friend and it felt awkward. When I started the public high school that September, The Fox was a year ahead of me, a junior. When I saw her, she wouldn't talk to me. We never had a fight, so to this day, I don't know what I did wrong. But I wish she would have told me then I could have done something to fix it. I wish more people, even in my own age bracket, would communicate better. Why is hate so much easier than working out the truth, which results in love?

Chapter 6

From day one, public high school was strange. They had a "smoking lounge" outside for the kids. Truth be told, the kids smoked cigarettes in the bathrooms and pot outside in the designated smoking lounge.

Some of these kids were nice and I tried pot with them. It wasn't my thing, so I didn't fit in with them. It was 1978, some had leftover hippie values. They just wanted to chill, and smoke weed.

In addition to the potheads, I made friends with straight kids too. ("Straight" back then meant you didn't drink or do drugs; it had nothing to do with sexuality). The straight kids were sweet and smart. They were into the drama club and the school newspaper. They had great bonds with each other. But I thought I wasn't brainy enough, so I didn't quite fit in with them either.

It seemed that everyone was either one way or the other. And it was hard to find my place. I liked make-up and I wore a lot of it. My mother had a friend who was a hairstylist. I instructed her to put heavy blonde highlights in my hair. I loved it. I liked to stand out. But that made me a "whore" to the kids in school. When I wore a pair of purple satin pants to school I was made fun of. Again, I was stuck in a place where people weren't very creative and only wore blue jeans. But one kid in my music class liked them and told me that's how girls in California dressed. That made me feel good. Temporarily.

Girls started "whore" rumors about me, but truth be told, I was heartbroken because a cute boy I wouldn't have sex with had just dumped me. All these girls had something against me and I didn't do anything to them. I was confused. I overheard someone say it was because I "laughed too much." This is what I wrote in my diary. I don't really remember laughing much at all back then.

Not finding a place to fit in started taking its toll on me again and I grew very insecure. No matter how many compliments I got on my looks (one girl friend said she'd give me a 9 on a scale of 1 to 10) if one person said something negative, that would bring me down several notches. I always scored myself a 3.

Then I started starving myself. Not in an anorexia way, just not eating until dinner time. This is actually very healthy if you do it in the right way, with lots of liquids or juicing. I didn't do it the right way. I'd have headaches in school every single day from not eating, then I'd come home and pig out on my grandmother's pasta dishes, with at least three slices of bread to dunk in the sauce. Eating this way, starving then eating a high carb dinner with zero or minimal protein because I hated meat, I was no longer able to concentrate on my work in school. My grandmother took valium to make her sleep. I started stealing them from her, so I could sleep too.

I told a male friend school. He confided in me that he tried a drug and drank and had a horrible experience. He made me promise him that I'd stop taking valium.

Here and there I made a few friends, but nothing significant or lasting (until my senior year). Though I did very nice things for my friends, like chipping in to get a girl a guitar for her birthday.

On the other side of the coin, I re-read my old diaries from this time and saw an ugliness in my writing. I started calling random people "dogs" and "scumbags," just as I was called in grade school. Not that I'd ever say it to their faces. I was just lashing out and hurting people with my pen … because I was hurt. I got into an awful habit of judging people for their looks because I was judged for my looks. If a pretty girl in school dated a guy who wasn't that good looking, I'd say things like, "What does she see in him?" without knowing the guy's personality.

In these very diaries I crossed out so many bad things I wrote about people, even if they were mean to me back then. I was truly regretful for that attitude I developed not only towards other people, but especially towards myself. I now referred to myself as a "loser." No matter how many compliments I'd get, I'd still believe I was a "dog."

All that said, I still went after the best-looking guys to date--and got them. But then once they were interested, I'd question if I was "good enough" for him. One day I'd feel confident, and one little thing would set me off, making me feel like the "scum" again. Like if a girl in the hallway gave me a dirty look. Maybe it wasn't even a dirty look. Perhaps she was deep in thought. That's not how I saw it though. Then every time I vowed to not put myself down anymore, I did it again. And again. And again.

In school there was a bit of a light at the end of the tunnel. I took Music Theory. I never played an instrument, but we did reports on musicians and learned about music. We had so much fun in the class. I made friends with a very nice guy named Chris. We lost touch after high school but reconnected on Facebook and drop each other a line from time to time. One day a boy in the class named John took perfume away from a girl in the class and sprayed it in Chris's hair. I had perfume in my purse, so I gave it to Chris, so he could spray John back. He did. Then John was trying to get the perfume away from me, but I wouldn't give it to him. We all had a laugh about that. Music Theory class was always fun.

One of my biggest problems, I think, was that I was too honest. After that guy Mike dumped me for not having sex with him, I tried sharing my hurt feelings with some girls in the bathroom at school. One of the older girls, with cigarette in tow, and super cute Candies heels, said, "Honey, you were too good for him. You'll meet someone else." This didn't stop me from pining for Mike. I told anyone who would listen about him. When I spoke of him, I included his last name, which was dumb. In grammar school, female students had loose lips about boys. In high school, you had to be very serious with someone before you could talk about them, it seemed. From school to school, all the rules were different, just like in real life. I never learned the rules fast enough. Who makes up these rules anyway? Is there a book for each town? Or is it all word of mouth. And why didn't I hear of these rules. Sigh ... I was never good with rules anyway.

So, turns out a girl from another school, who was friends with someone in my school, got wind that Mike was once my boyfriend and now she liked him. Knowing I still liked him, she spitefully bragged to someone I knew that he was coming to see her perform in a talent show. She knew it would get back to me.

A glutton for punishment, I went to the talent show just to see Mike again, even if he was with someone else. I wasn't being stalkerish, I just wanted to see him.

Before the girl was about to go on, I saw her standing by the stage and she looked beautiful. She had long, golden-brown hair, curled at the bottom. She was wearing nothing but a body suit, and tights.

Then, I couldn't believe my eyes. There was Mike in the audience. He noticed me too and came over. He put his arm around me, in a friendly way. We watched the girl perform with our arms around each other.

So, the girl is onstage, dancing to a disco tune, "Shake Your Groove Thing" and whipping her hair around. Then she spotted

Mike and me. In the middle of the song, she stopped dancing and ran off the stage crying.

It was hilarious. She got her instant karma for trying to hurt me. Mike tried to get back with me that night, but I still wouldn't have sex with him. So of course, he got mad and that was that. Those teenage boys and their hormones!

I got over Mike a month or so later when I met another boy at a party, I'll call him Aaron. He was cute with long blonde hair. Everyone knew who he was. He was very popular with the young ladies. I made sure he knew I was interested and within a week we were an item. Unlike Mike, Aaron was very slow in the sex department. We spent the next few months just kissing anywhere we couldn't be seen. He went to an all boy school and our time together was limited to a few nights per week, somewhere between 4 and 8 p.m.

What I really liked about Aaron was that he was a musician. He later went on to become successful in the music business. I loved going to see his band practice a few times per week. I hosted their first performance in my basement in Cedar Grove. It was the first party I had since I got in trouble at my seventh-grade party. I dressed to the nines with my satin pants, a silk shirt, and a big hat. I crimped my hair too, which was the style of the late 1970s, though not really hitting mainstream until the 1980s. I was so proud announcing the band. All my friends came and had a great time. People were talking about the show for days.

In school I wrote on the bathroom wall "Maryanne + Aaron." This was no big deal. All the girls wrote their names with their boyfriend's name on bathroom walls or they'd carve the names on desks. But I was a target because so many girls had crushes on Aaron. I'd go back to the bathroom and see my name crossed out. I'd rewrite it. Then the same thing. Then I wrote, "Face the fact, he's my boyfriend."

Next time they wrote "Aaron is a fag and Maryanne is a space case."

We all know that when haters hate, there is no changing their minds. I was wise enough to know this at 15. What could I do to convince people to be on my side? Nothing. I was a target.

Another thing girls didn't like about me was that I wore a lot of make-up and they didn't. Not in my suburban school. But I didn't want to be boring like them. I wore heavy eye make-up like the all-girl band, The Runaways. A guy in school told me I look like I belonged in that band. That made my year because they were all pretty.

One day a girl was drinking alcohol from a bottle in one of my classes. The teacher looked over and to avoid getting caught, the girl put the bottle in *my* bag! I almost got in trouble, but I told the teacher it wasn't mine, which was the truth.

As I'm writing this book, I just became the spokesperson for the Coalition for Human Condition and was invited to speak on anti-bullying. A teacher onboard said that bullies seem to target the strong people. I never thought of it that way. But it's true. Cliques are a weak link. Those who stand on their own are strong. This not only bothers people, it offends them. People who flock together can't understand the individual mindset.

So, what did I do at this point? I entertained myself. I didn't give in by feeling like a victim, I went along with their silly game and played the role they assigned. I acted like a nut. And it was fun.

Simultaneously, The Sex Pistols were doing the same thing to audiences--playing with them. I was not yet exposed to The Sex Pistols, other than the fact that Sid Vicious just died. Even the coolest radio stations in NYC didn't play their records. But I found their record, two years after it was first released, with a green $3.99 sticker on it. I only heard snippets of their songs on the radio, so I blindly brought the album. And I loved every song.

Here's an example of how I played with people. After Sid Vicious died, I became curious about punk rock. I started putting safety pins on my bag. One day a girl, who never spoke to me before, needed a safety pin for something. She asked me for one.

I said, "I don't have a safety pin." Obviously, they were all over my bag. Then the very next day, I approached her and said, "Here's a safety pin." Of course, she didn't need one the next day.

Another example, one time I was using my mirror. A girl who always bothered me asked, "Do you have a mirror?"

I said, "No," even though she knew I had one. I'd make people know they weren't going to use me.

Around this time, I met George, who went to another school in West Milford, New Jersey. But he came to my area to visit his family. George was very much into music. By now Aaron's mother had broken us up and forbid him to see me. She never liked me for some reason. I was available to date George and I did.

On our first date we went to see the movie, "Hair." The next night he invited me over for dinner at his father's. Warren Hall, lived in a townhouse, The Claridge House in Verona owned by his girlfriend Lori Burton (Cicala). Lori was a famous singer and songwriter. She sang back up with May Pang and John Lennon on his song, "Number 9 Dream." During dinner, I spotted the gold record, "Number 9 Dream" hanging in the dining room.

Lori also co-wrote the song, "Ain't Gonna Eat Out My Heart Anymore" which was recorded by The Rascals, as well as one of my favorite bands at the time, Angel. (Many years later, one of my dreams came true when my husband and I met their guitarist Punky Meadows after a show at B.B. Kings in New York).

I was impressed meeting Lori. She was easy going and gorgeous. She wore her hair in a long wedge style which accented her perfect cheekbones. When she smiled, her face lit up. I didn't say much, but I felt perfectly comfortable in her presence.

A few weeks later George told me he shared with Lori that I was having problems with other kids in school, mainly because of how I looked with my heavy make-up and hair highlighted bleach blonde (which is now so common with kids today).

"So, what's a little bit of eye make-up?" Lori said, defending me.

I was secretly proud that this beautiful person I highly admired was sticking up for me. I took her words to heart and started feeling proud of who I was; a young girl who emulated the female muses and musicians of my generation. Not high school girls who hid in cliques and bullied others to make themselves feel better.

George was very wise for his age. He said that the guys made fun of me because they couldn't date me. And the girls made fun of me because they're jealous. They wouldn't let me in their clique because I was "too good" for them.

He was right. I was too good because I wasn't into gossip and putting people down. I just wanted to listen to music, talk about music, and have a good time. People had their deluded version of me because they never got to know me.

I promised George I wouldn't put myself down anymore, but I also wouldn't call myself "beautiful" as he called me. That was a bit extreme.

As a side note, to this day I converse with Lori on Facebook. Like myself, she's an animal lover and does so much to support animal rights. We always bond over how some terrible people treat animals.

I DON'T WANT TO BE LIKE YOU

Chapter 7

My grandmother and grandfather were getting divorced, so we had to downsize and leave the beautiful house in Cedar Grove. We moved into a two-bedroom apartment in Little Falls, New Jersey. I was so depressed. I had to get rid of so much of my stuff, like my comic book collection. Then during the move, I didn't have a phone for a few days. The first day George was over he said it was "weird" and he missed our old house.

It was April 1979. That summer I'd be 16. My body was changing. My breasts were growing. I was gaining weight, which was of course normal for a teenager. I was still on the thin side, yet I felt my body was "disgusting." Boys had raging hormones and it was the norm to hear them talk about tits all the time. My male friends were no longer fun. Some of them started getting negative on me calling me names like "cunt" and talking shit about George. These were kids I had over my house too. It really hurt that they turned on me just because I wouldn't date them. They'd only talk to me if they wanted to use me for a ride home. I now lived in their area and my grandmother picked me up from school every day.

Girls were also fickle, and I couldn't figure out who my friends were. Some days they'd talk to me. Some days they wouldn't. And they never told me why they were mad at me. I'd just get dirty looks. I was always so forgiving back then. Once I was someone's friend, I'd go along with their moods and accept them. Sometimes I wish I still had that innocence inside me but being too trusting isn't a good thing. However, I can look back and admire myself for not having hate in my heart for friends that turned on me. Nowadays, I won't put myself in that position, but I do pray and send positive vibes to my enemies.

A strange thing that happened was getting bullied at a carnival. I was with my sister and another friend. We were having the time of our lives just doing teenage things like going on the rides and joking around. For no reason at all three girls from our high school, one who had a reputation for being the toughest, started giving us the finger and verbally abusing us. We stood up for ourselves and fought back. It's so bizarre that girls would want to start trouble in such a happy place as a carnival. It was absurd to me then, and it's still weird to me now. It just didn't make sense, except that maybe they thought they'd get away with it because teachers weren't around. By now it got to a point where I started to have dreams about being bullied; and the carnival scenario was relived in my dream. I just couldn't get away from it.

While the girls continued to bully me, the guys continued to ask me out. It got back to me that one who I thought was a good friend lied about me and said we were an item for about a day, then I left him for someone else. That was very uncool. What was worse was the ones who lied and said they didn't have girlfriends, but they did. I wouldn't date guys who had girlfriends; and over the summer it was easy for them to lie.

I had broken up with George right before summer. I never wanted to get too close to anyone because I was so fearful I wasn't good enough and I'd get hurt. So, I'd keep things light. Also, that summer, my family took a long road and we visited 22 states. With a stack of music magazines in the back of the van, I was good to go as we drove across the United States. We drove through Death Valley to visit Las Vegas; saw three major cities in California: Los Angeles (and Hollywood), San Francisco, and San Diego; traveled down into caverns in Texas; saw the salt mines of Utah; visited Elvis Presley's home; and saw jazz artists in the streets of New Orleans. Our final night was in Atlantic City, New Jersey. Atlantic City is known for being a gambling resort. I never liked gambling, but rather the boardwalk and seeing shows. After visiting 22 states, New Jersey was and always will be my favorite. We have everything, beautiful beaches, mountains, cities, and suburbs. There is so much culture and unique charm from town to town. You can never be bored in New Jersey. The best of everything is just a car ride away.

Chapter 8

When I was a junior at the public school, the bullying got worse. I tried without much success to get out of classes where I was harassed. One time a girl bothered me so much, and I was ahead of her as we exited the classroom. I slammed the door right in her face to make my point, "just leave me the hell alone."

I'd go to the nurse's office and talk to the nurses about my problems. They were compassionate, yet nothing was ever done. There was a new kid in my homeroom named Mark and we became friends. I was telling him about the bullies in school and a janitor overhead me.

The janitor said, "You're good looking. You have a complex." (As if bullies only picked on ugly girls.) I was flattered that an adult complimented my looks but frustrated that none of the adults in the school went the extra mile to take care of the situation. Nowadays they have video cameras in some schools and bullies can be caught on film and addressed. But this was the 1970s and now I was beginning to have nightmares about being harassed in school.

When you're verbally harassed constantly, it takes its toll on you. Imagine being called something derogatory, by not just one, but many people. Eventually you break down and drop to their level. That's what happened to me. For every girl who called me a name, I now had names for them. "Pretty is as pretty does" is an old-fashioned saying. So, I had no problems calling ugly-spirited girls ugly names. An ugly girl at the carnival who bullied me was now "Mole Head" because she had a big head and a mean face like a mole. Another was called "The Nose" for her oversized nose. Another was called "Flatsy" for being skinny. Another was "Wonder Tooth" because she had a crooked front tooth. (And I have a crooked front tooth too; as well as a lump on my nose; and except for my butt I was skinny also; which goes to show how shameless I was in insulting people!)

Looking back, this was so out of character for me. Anyone who has known me since my 20s, I'm the girl everyone feels comfortable around. I have no ego and am like a comfortable old shoe. I am known amongst my friends for seeing the beauty in everyone. One of my friends once said, "I can have messy hair, or a pimple and you still see me as beautiful." It is true. I feel all women are beautiful.

Any color, any race, any size or shape, or any age. However, when someone is a rotten person, I will not see them as anything good. Ugly goes straight to the bone.

It's like when you meet a cute guy. If he has a great personality and a great sense of humor, you will see him as even cuter. Perhaps even a prince! But if he's an asshole, you'll lose interest. That's why sometimes a guy that's not so good looking will score an amazing girlfriend. As my grandmother would put it, "He has a good line of shit."

That's the crass old school Italian way to say, "He's got a fab personality." And the world could certainly use a little more of that nowadays. Personalities today are so robotic. But that's another story.

What really bothered me back then was I could never find a true high school friend. A girl I'll call Kay would pal around with me. We ate over each other's houses, went roller skating, went to the beach, and even celebrated our birthdays together. The problem was, she had a bit of a mean streak when it came to me. She was jealous that I attracted more boys than she did. Eventually she'd start giving me little digs. If I said a guy was cute, she'd say, "Oh, I don't think so," as if she was so superior.

Throughout sophomore and most of junior year, I had very long hair and did what was called "frosting." It gave my hair an ash/gray effect, like many young girls do today. It was a very modern look. Too modern for the girls in boring suburban New Jersey. But one day Mole Head copied my look. Now she had the ash/gray hair too.

Because this bitch always started trouble, then copied my look, I made a catty comment to Kay that Mole Head didn't look good with *my* look.

Kay said, "Oh, (Note, every sentence of hers began with the dramatic 'Oh') I don't think it looks that bad." Shame, she couldn't even defend me. She was afraid of the bullies. This made me realize Kay was not a good friend. I soon cut ties with her and never talked to her again. It's Romy & Michele 101. You don't praise people who bully your friends!

I'd like to pause here and say that during three years of continuous bullying at school, it never stopped me from doing wonderful things, like dating, bowling, going for pizza, and going to the movies. But my creativity in school was stifled because I was so stressed all the time. While I was a good student at Neuman Prep, at the public school, I was just getting by. When I ran into students from Neuman Prep at the shopping mall, I'd end up talking to them for almost an hour!

There was always that little bit of light, but most days my diary entries simply read, "Life sucks."

Chapter 9

During my junior year at high school, I took a part-time job. My stepfather was a police officer in Paterson, New Jersey. He also owned a soda/coffee shop. I was hired to work behind the counter. One of the cutest things was when a little boy said to me, "Lady, can I kiss you?"

I really enjoyed the job. Chatting with customers and playing pinball on my breaks. But I didn't last at the job for long. I didn't get along with my stepfather. He'd put me down in front of customers. Then when some of the local boys verbally fought with me, he sided with them. It was a shame no one realized what a good person I was. One of the boys who started trouble with me later had a serious kidney infection and I visited him in the hospital. I was so compassionate, wishing it was me instead. I overlooked that he previously started trouble for me.

And another weird thing was, even though no one from my high school went to the soda shop, they all knew I worked there! Brit, who started all that trouble for me in grade school, went around telling everyone where I worked. When I worked, I was alone several hours during the night, so I was always on guard that someone from school was going to come in and harass me.

However, I was starting to become less introverted and more personable. I had no problem making friends. But finding friends who were a good fit continued to be a challenge. Most teenagers in the 1970s were self-absorbed. Today, you see young girls really bonding, hugging each other, taking selfies together. I never had that. I was always exposed to young women being at each other's throats and talking bad about each other. Or simply being in their own little worlds.

For example, I took music theory class throughout my years at the public school. It was always an easy "A" for the semester. There was a fat kid in the class that no one liked. I don't remember why. He never hurt anyone. Maybe he was just different, like I was. A guy who was my friend in class wanted to write a letter to the fat kid and tell him what he thought of him.

I told him that was a "stupid" thing to do. Even when I was in the position to be a bully, I wouldn't do it. I could never hurt someone for no reason. This is where the disconnect was. If another kid was doing something I didn't want to do, I had to stay true to myself. Another time a guy who had a crush on me wanted to beat up a guy who bullied me. I told him "don't." I wasn't about violence.

However, getting pushed to the limit, I now wasn't above pulling a mean prank on a mean girl. Early in my junior year I became friends with a girl I'll call Vicky. She was gorgeous, had a lot of boyfriends, and was tough. So tough that she once put another girl in the hospital by beating her. For some reason Vicky liked me. We were friends up until our 20s. Again, not an ideal friendship. We had our ups and downs too.

There was a girl in our record keeping class who always harassed me for wearing too much make-up. One day before she got to class, Vicky and I put chalk on her chair. When she got up, she had chalk all over her pants. It was funny and harmless. And it was nothing compared to the verbal abuse and death threats via obscene phone calls that I got.

One time I was in a class and there was a substitute teacher. Whenever that happened, kids became very unruly. So, this was my day to be harassed by an entire classroom. I simply walked out.

A pretty girl named Pam stood up for me and addressed the classroom. "I don't blame her for walking out. How would you like it if everyone called you a 'space case'?" She silenced them.

Then she came after me and said, "Come back so you don't get in trouble."

I took a deep breath and came back to class.

"Maryanne, you came back!" Pam said. Her face lit up. She was proud of me.

A few years ago, I found her on Face Book and thanked her. I offered to take her to lunch. We met at the Tick Tock Diner. I brought her flowers too. We got along great and had the waiter take a picture of us together. We saw each other a few more times and keep in touch. Pam is very successful today.

Another time a girl just started picking on me. I simply said to her, "Fuck off." And she changed her attitude!

I was now listening to The Who and The Sex Pistols. Two different types of music – one rock, the other punk. But both empowering bands with messages. This music was making me come out of my shell and fight back. A little bit, not always.

When I first started wearing contact lenses, it took a long time to get used to them. I had a backup pair of glasses, which were tinted dark. They were like a big pair of rock star sunglasses. I wore them to school one day and a boy laughed right in my face. I ran to the bathroom, took my glasses off, put my contact lenses back in and cried. I was so fed up, I walked out of class.

It was winter; and a snowstorm started. I had about a 10- to 15-minute walk home, up a big hill. A guy pulled over and asked me if I needed a ride.

I told him I was almost home, but I naively added, "I could use a friend to talk to."

I later learned he was 26-years-old, which is ancient to a teenager. He lived by himself in another apartment complex, near the one I lived in with my grandmother, great-grandmother, and sister. He invited me in for coffee. But then he wanted to smoke pot. I declined. Then he wanted a "kiss for Christmas." I was terrified and bolted for the door. I ran out of the complex. He followed me in his car.

"You're going to get all wet," he said to me. I kept running.

Then another guy pulled over and asked if I needed a ride. I declined. I learned my lesson.

When I got home, I lied to my grandmother and told her I went out for a recess break and slipped in the snow, so I wanted to come home and change my clothes. I didn't have the heart to tell her that a fellow student laughed at me and it got the best of me.

"Just stay home," she said. And of course, I did.

I DON'T WANT TO BE LIKE YOU

Chapter 10

Today there's a word for it--cutting.

I did this from time to time when I was 15 and 16. I made small cuts in my skin. It empowered me. I'd do it with a razor blade. One time I made a boy's initial. Another time I made a heart. Both left scars which have long faded; one now replaced with a tattoo. Another time I just made three deep slashes on the side of my wrist. They took forever to fade, but now that I'm in my 50s there are no scars.

When I was sick and had to get a needle in my arm at the doctor's office, I loved it. Physical pain took away the emotional. I can understand why teenagers today cut. Fortunately, it was something I outgrew.

One night I had a dream that I stood up to an entire classroom and asked them, "What did I ever do to you?" As much as I've grown and come out of my shell, I still didn't have the nerve to do that. Especially since it was so many kids against just me.

February 2, 1980 was one year from the date that Sid Vicious died. I felt bad for the guy when he died and connected with him being a misfit. I didn't take into consideration that he was a heroin addict and was on trial for killing his girlfriend Nancy Spungen.

It's still a mystery whether Sid Vicious killed Nancy Spungen, but it is a fact that he strangled a cat, so I have no respect for him at all. People who torture animals are disgusting. I did not know this until I recently saw a movie about his life. One of his friends saw him do it. Why didn't he stop him?!

But as a misfit teen, I was relating to another misfit. When Sid Vicious died on February 2, 1979, I soon afterward wrote a poem about him. On February 2, 1980, I was brave enough to show it to the kids in my music class. Some of them liked it! And the music teacher started putting music to it. It was one of the happier entries in my diary for 1980. Then a few weeks later I read more of my poems in Family Development class--and everyone in the class loved them! (In later years, I began my writing career by doing open mics reading poetry I wrote. Both my poetry and deliverance were more than well received.)

Around this time, a cute guy in one of my classes liked me. I'll call him Max. We had a lot in common. Both of us liked punk rock and we got along great. I was crushing on him for some time and I'd stay up all night thinking about him. Then he finally took me out. We did a few light-hearted fun things together like hanging out at the mall and kissing in his car, parked in a graveyard. That's as far as it went. He was a real gentleman.

The next day there was an event in the school auditorium. He sat right next to me. His ex-girlfriend, I'll call her Cheryl, saw us together and started crying her eyes out, making a real scene. After the event I watched Max approach her.

"Stop it," he said, as he gave her a light push on her shoulder. "I don't like you anymore and we're not going out."

Soon afterwards, word got out about that. Then Brit was at it again. She started a rumor that I had sex with Max. That was not true. She announced loudly to anyone who was listening, "I can't believe he stooped so low. Poor Cheryl was so hurt. Somebody's gonna beat her [me] up for doing that!"

Naturally the dumb bitch blamed me for everything ... Max didn't have anything to do with hurting his ex-girlfriend. The one-sided way girls and women think sometimes is just pitiful!

I later slipped Max a note explaining what happened. I knew if I spoke aloud to him I'd start crying.

He read the note. All he had to say was, "Don't worry about it."

That night I stayed home and cried. But I wasn't just crying for myself. I was crying because the girl was hurt. I called a girlfriend I'll call Terri and told her how bad I felt. She was good friends with Max and thought very highly of him.

Terri said, "Don't feel bad. Be happy about it. You're better than her. She's jealous." Then she added, "You couldn't pick a nicer person to go out with."

Max was friends with Terri, but he was also friends with the guys and girls who harassed me. The next day I saw him in school and he was being very nice to me. Then he called me that night and told me he got a job and we wouldn't get to see each other much. I was smart enough to know it was a lie. Young people are often influenced by their friends, so I can only imagine what these losers in school said bad about me. And Max was a coward for going along with it. Now I was the one hurt.

That night I cried again and ended up calling George for comfort.

"It's a wonder you don't get a nervous breakdown," he said.

The next day after gym I was changing in the locker room and Brit took a picture of me in my underwear. I was terrified, wondering what she was going to do with the picture. God bless my sister Kim. She put my mind at ease when she said, "Don't worry, you have nice legs." Great point! Underwear is no different than a bikini!

And that night Max called me again. This time to tell me he was back with Cheryl. I decided I suffered enough with all the bullshit and got over it quick. Max was nothing special anymore. Plus, I was preoccupied with the fact that I had tickets to see The Clash!

A few weeks earlier I had seen the movie "Foxes" starring Cherie Currie of The Runaways and got my hair cut like hers. My mother also let me stay home from school a few days because I was so stressed out. And this was normally unheard of in my family. My mother was one of the hardest, most dedicated workers I've known in my 50-something years. I took after her developing the same type of work ethic. Looking back, the bullying and harassment, especially now with Brit back in the picture, was horrific.

At this point, my mother took it upon herself to go to the school and tell them how Brit was continuously picking on me.

The night after the concert, Terri called me and told me that Cheryl wanted to call me and apologize, but Max wouldn't give her my phone number.

I went back to school the following day and Brit pushed me, demanding to know why I was trying to get her "screwed." I guess someone in faculty told her to stop bothering me, but it backfired and now it was worse.

I didn't answer her and simply walked away. Two periods later she found me again in the hallway and pushed me into the boy's room and held me against the wall. A whole gang of kids stood watching. It was pathetic. This tall, husky almost-woman person, who was a year older than me had me up against a wall. And I was small, 5'2" and 105 pounds at most. I was afraid to do anything to her; I didn't want to get in trouble. I got away and stood near a classroom so maybe a teacher would come out and see what was going on. Brit got scared and went away, as did the crowd of kids. What cowards.

I went home and cried again. And listened to The Clash.

When I went to school the next day, Cheryl did apologize. Nevertheless, I was extremely stressed in school. I'd forget to bring home books to study for tests. Someone carved my name in one of the wooden desks, saying that I was a "tramp." I continued to steal my grandmother's valium pills; and sneak wine or whatever liquor we had in the house, to ease my pain a bit.

But something magical was happening. I was becoming empowered by punk rock music, especially The Clash and The Sex Pistols. I started dressing punk rock, which back then was mild. I simply wore ripped jeans and put safety pins on my t-shirts and bag.

Sometimes when I had money I'd buy something more "outrageous" like a pink zebra stripped spandex shirt. One day I was wearing that shirt and my former friend Kay started mocking me and called me a "space case." She was with a few friends who chimed in.

Once again Pam came to my rescue. "Are you calling her a space cadet? That's the trouble with you--your mouths!" Then she really went off on a tangent defending me. She left them speechless.

I couldn't thank her enough. "You're too much!" I said. This go 'round I wasn't too shy to express my gratitude. At that very moment I wished I could do something for her. But, like I wrote earlier, years later I made good on what she did for me.

Though it wasn't much later that I didn't need anyone to defend me. I started mouthing off to anyone who talked shit to me or about me. I developed a smart-ass attitude. Punk rock galvanized me. Now I was the one with "the mouth." The Sex Pistols gave me great ideas for insults. Borrowed from them, I'd call assholes "middle class twats." I started carrying scissors around with me, so I could threaten anyone who bothered me.

I also started speaking in a British accent. I even fooled a substitute teacher who asked me, "How long are you going to be in the States?"

I started hanging around at a record store called Looney Tunes in Wayne, New Jersey. This is where I got all my 45-rpm records and long-playing albums, as well as buttons to put on my clothes. The buttons had names and pictures of the bands I loved. My collection of buttons was growing.

A dumb comment I got was, "You don't have to advertise that you like punk rock."

Yes, I did.

And now random people were giving me safety pins. A kid in my history class gave me a Sex Pistols button that his friend found. Even Max gave me a Sid Vicious lock. "It looks better on you than it does on me," he said.

I had an acoustic guitar that I destroyed with a pair of scissors. I carved names of the bands I liked into the wood: The Jam, The Clash, Sex Pistols and PIL.

One of the teen magazines at the time had a music match up. You'd answer a questionnaire about music and they'd match you up with a pen pal. I ended up being pen pals with a girl from Oklahoma I'll call Tina. She was beautiful. Tall and thin with super long blonde hair. She shared with me that she was having problems with bullying in school too. Girls threatened to pour honey on her head. And on her last day of the school year they destroyed her car. I was so protective of my pen pal. It angered me to hear such sad things.

One day a random girl pulled my hair.

"Fuck off," I told her and then slapped her in the face.

"Don't slap me!" she yelled and slapped me back.

I reported her to the guidance counselor and she got 10 days' detention. And my punishment was that I had to talk to the school psychiatrist, but he was on the phone when I went to his office. Both the school nurse and the guidance counselor insisted that I went out of my way to be different. They said I shouldn't wear safety pins and buttons because it was "offensive."

I retaliated by saying that it was offensive to me that other kids looked so boring. (Meanwhile, if I went to a Ramones concert, people would want to take my picture because they liked the way I was dressed!)

The following day I stayed home from school again for a few days. Back then there was no such thing as Caller ID so I'd get random anonymous messages from time to time. They were often from guys who were crushing on me. One night I picked up the phone and heard weird noises and synthesizer notes. Then in a distorted robotic voice someone said, "This is not the end."

The threat was scary, but I made it to the end of junior year alive. Nevertheless, just a few days before school was out, there was more bizarre randomness. I was on my way to a senior graduation party. It was a summer night, so I walked. Another senior saw me walking and drove slowly to follow me in her car. Then she screamed out the window, "You fucking whore!" Interesting, this same girl ended up in a dance class I took when I was 19. When I first saw she was in my class, I was nervous, but she was actually a very nice girl. Maybe she had the wrong "whore."

That summer I ran into three of the grade school bullies while I was hanging out at the local Quick Chek. They asked me if I wanted a ride. I refused three times. They kept saying, "C'mon it's cool. We'll give you a ride." I finally agreed to it. And it was cool.

Chapter 11

For my 17th birthday my mother got me a leather jacket! It was a true punk rock status symbol. Every now and then I met random punk rockers that would chat with me and treat me like a human being. At Great Adventure (known as Six Flags in other states), at carnivals, or at the mall. Even at a local pharmacy a young guy started talking to me because I had on a Sid & Nancy button. He told me about the New York City clubs he went to.

But school bullies always seemed to find me, even during summer vacation. My family lived on the second floor of an apartment complex. If I looked out my bedroom window, there was a cellar access door. Sometimes teens from the complex would go there and hang out, sitting on the access door. I could hear them talking from my bedroom.

One day I went to the access door with my sister and we discovered somebody wrote with brown spray paint "Punk sucks!" That was obviously directed at me. And now my sister too because she liked punk rock at the time. We found white spray paint in our home, sprayed off "Sucks" and just left "Punk."

While kids today constantly get harassed on the internet, back then we had anonymous telephone calls. There wasn't Caller I.D., but you could trace the calls. However, people would call from a pay phone. I had a "secret admirer" who would call from time to time. One day I kept him on the phone to try to figure out who it was, but he was getting nasty with me, telling me to talk dirty to him.

The operator kept getting on the phone, "Please deposit ten cents."

The first time I was ever stalked on the internet, I was reminded of these pathetic "invisible" people who made anonymous calls. Cowards!

Right before my senior year in high school I started exploring NYC and Greenwich Village. In 1980 there were so many punk rockers in the streets. And nobody bothered me for being a punk rocker. No one would bat an eye at you. It felt like peace to me; a sanctuary. There was a super cool record store called Bleeker Bob's. There was also Trash & Vaudeville on St. Mark's Place. And many other cool, indie places to shop. And on the "other side of the world" all along the Jersey shore, punk rock was a big deal. You always saw punk rockers at the shore. Earlier that summer I went to Wildwood with my family. We saw a great Elvis impersonator. My mother went back to see him again in August and returned with a t-shirt for me that had barb wire printed on it. A punk scene was everywhere. Retail stores really tapped into that.

Then back to school in September, from day one it was a nightmare. A girl kicked me in the leg for no reason at all. I just looked at her.

She said, "I'm sorry, I really am. I didn't mean that." How can you not "mean" to kick someone in the leg?

Her friend said, "She meant to kick you in the ear. And spit on you. Punks get into that."

I said nothing, left school and came home. In fact, I cut school often during my senior year. The advisors couldn't get my class schedule straight. I was trying to arrange classes that didn't have bullies in them. Guidance counselors would say, "Just ignore them." But how could you ignore people kicking you and threatening to spit on you? So, I'd cut classes and go home early or just stay home period--and sleep. I still got a "B" grade on my composition on The Sex Pistols, which was great!

Life was different in *my* world. I was always going to see live music, both in New Jersey and New York City. I spent time hanging out down the Jersey shore. And back then there were midnight movies. One night I went to see "The Doors Are Open" with a bunch of friends from other schools. Some were already in college.

I was in such a good mood. I saw one of the bullies in the girl's bathroom and said, "How are you doing?" She was dumbstruck. Shame though, it could have been an opportunity to be friends. Can't say I didn't try.

Then someone tripped me in the aisle. I didn't know who it was at the time, but I later found out, from George, who was at The Doors movie. It was this girl who was always jealous of me. Whenever I talked to someone in her group who I was friends with, she'd run away because she didn't want to be bothered with me. It was all so silly. She also said to George, who didn't go to our school, "You think Maryanne's so great now, you should see her in school when everyone hates her."

It was all so petty to me, really.

It was only two months into the senior year and I started going to nightclubs. It was easy to get in with fake I.D. I was 16, but could pass for 18, which was the drinking age at the time. I ran into two kids who graduated a year ahead of me. They were now dressed punk and wearing a lot of make-up. And they were being nice. It was great. If someone was cool to me, I was cool back. I never sought revenge on a bully or anyone who was indifferent to me. Then I'd see other bullies who were now sporting pink hair to be "punk" and they still hated me.

One of my high school moments of glory was when a guidance counselor's 13-year-old daughter called me up asking for advice because she wanted to be a punk rocker for Halloween; and borrow something from my wardrobe. And random people still thought I was from London.

Out of the blue a friend of a friend came to the conclusion that I "hated" him. I didn't. I liked him and considered him a friend. It was the first situation where a person thought I hated them, instead of the usual, them hating on me. While now, I would feel horrible if someone thought that, back then I secretly felt empowered. But I made sure the friend made it clear that I liked the other friend.

One friend made a list of 50 of my good points (and I did the same for him). The first one on the list was "Is cool." I was surprised to read that but agreed to myself that I did develop into a cool chick. I was happy with myself.

Number 5 was another thing I never heard before was that I knew how to present myself with clothes and make-up. That would be called "stylish." Today strangers and young people still tell me I am "stylish." I owe a lot of it to emulating punk rock styles. That taught me not to go with fashions, but to wear what I really like. During the lean times in my career, I always put myself together with a budget. But I'll never forget spending part of a large work bonus on a metallic blue vinyl mini dress for a magazine party.

Number 16 was that I accept people the way they are.

Number 22 was that I listen to people's thoughts and ideas.

As much as young people are selfish, and I'll be the first to admit I was too, I'm so happy to go back to my old diaries and read some of this stuff. Ever since I started writing this book, I kept telling my husband, "I was such a good kid!"

When Halloween finally rolled around, I got wind of it that many in my school were dressing as punk rockers. Or as I wrote in my diary, "They are gonna attempt to be punks."

So, naturally I one-upped them. I came to school wearing a

Lynyrd Skynyrd t-shirt that I borrowed from a friend. Lynyrd Skynyrd is a country rock band, who I thought was boring at the time. I never liked their music until I heard their song "Free Bird" in Rob Zombie movie later in life. Then it put a whole new twist on it.

I figured everyone was going to expect me to go "all out" as a punk rocker on Halloween, so I fooled them. I wore the t-shirt, jeans, a country hat, and I put a red bandana in my jeans pocket. And I didn't wear make-up.

It was just as I expected. People came up to me and said, "I thought you were going to go all out today!" But what I didn't expect was how many people told me how pretty I was without make-up. And that I looked good as one of them.

When I went to a party at night, I dressed as one of the Sleaze Sisters from the cult movie, "Times Square." I wore a garbage bag as a dress over pink spandex pants, with Converse All-Star sneakers. Three other girls showed up dressing the same!

A few days later something happened that later changed my whole life. I went to the mall with my mother, her girlfriend, and my sister Kim, but we all went our separate ways. I got a music newspaper and sat on a bench to flip through it. I was wearing a Gary Neuman t-shirt.

I was distracted when someone said, "Excuse me, could I see your shirt?"

I was afraid to look up from the newspaper because I thought it was going to be some jerk making fun of my t-shirt. I looked up slowly and saw two of the most outrageous looking guys in my area. They had super long dark hair with the sides bleach blonde. They wore snakeskin boots, spandex pants, and lots of buttons like I did. They looked more like glitter/glam rockers than punk rockers.

"Oh … Hi!" I said.

They both smiled, as if they knew my thoughts. Then they showed me their Gary Neuman buttons. We had all seen the show a few weeks prior. After some more small talk about all the bands we liked, I asked them if they were in a band.

Yes, they were; the band was called Pharoah. In later years they were successful, signed to a record label and even had a video on MTV. During one of their reunions, I really hit it off with their bass player Dennis Lords, and we ended up marrying. This was later in life. Dennis and I were both in our 40s, and still very young looking and very young spirited. We've now been together a total of 12 years and are still very much in love.

I was also part of Pharoah's stage show, temporarily. I'd dress up in lingerie, garter belt and stockings, and give the lead singer, Karl DeKira his guitar. It was cute and mild compared to what the other girls in the band did after me.

But, back to that day ... it was both Karl and Richard that were there at the mall. Richard later changed his name to Rik Fabio. One of them, I forgot which, told me I was the best thing they've seen at the mall and that nobody likes them. They had issues with people too because of how they looked. I exchanged numbers with Karl and we kept in touch.

A few nights later a girl in one of my classes was talking about "transvestites at the mall." I knew she was speaking about Karl and Richard because she was looking over at me as she said it. So obviously she saw them talking to me. By calling straight guys who were friendly with me "transvestites" it was her way of letting me know she disapproved of them and she wanted to make me feel bad. This truly illustrated the ignorance and intolerance of school kids in the late 1970s living in the suburbs. It was no wonder the two gay kids I was acquainted with kept it a secret.

Anyway, I said something back to the girl to put her in her place. And, of course I was the one who got caught by the teacher and had to get my seat changed. When I speak to others who were bullied in school, they often agree that the teachers took the side of the bullies in many instances. I saw this in my later adult years too, with people in a place of authority trying to be "in" with what they assumed to be the "cool crowd," who were in reality just scared sheep.

One day I was innocently walking to my locker and a senior boy threw his shop goggles at me but missed. I picked the goggles up and threw them back, hitting him in the leg. Then he threw the goggles at my head and hit me.

"Fucking asshole!" I said to him.

For once there was justice. Two male teachers caught him; and yelled at him. I also learned he got suspended.

Then another guy picked on me and I kicked him in the leg. Two days later I caught him showing his scar to everyone. This one I named "Tit Eyes" because he had huge eyes that bulged out like big boobs.

A few years later when I was around 22-years-old, I ran into Tit

Eyes in a bar. He was trying to pick me up. I was cordial, and we ended up having a nice conversation. All was forgiven on both ends. I left by accidentally saying, "It was nice talking to you Tit Eyes." I referred to him as Tit Eyes so much in high school, I didn't know his real name!

He just smiled. It was all good.

The Pretenders was another one of my favorite bands and I always wore a beautiful necklace that read "The Pretenders." It was given to me by a friend. One day I was daydreaming, playing with the necklace that I wore on my neck. Out of the blue a guy in school pushed me really hard, causing me to pull on the necklace and break the gold chain.

"Fucking asshole!" I said to him.

"Are you talking to me?"

"Yeah."

Then three of his friends appeared out of nowhere, just like in the movies. They all started yelling at me.

I started walking away then a male teacher came by. I told him, "You should supervise the hall."

All the boys got scared and ran away. I started crying. I was so upset about the necklace.

Whenever I first told my husband how I was bullied by boys in school he couldn't believe it. He said, "What kind of animals did you go to school with? In our school the boys never picked on girls."

I hated my school so much. For spite, one day a girlfriend and I taped a photo on a wall of a well-hung stud that we cut out of *Playgirl*. The next time we passed that wall, someone had taken it down already. But we'll never know if it was a teacher or a student.

Chapter 12

While I was a senior, my younger sister Kim was a freshman. One of her freshman friends was getting picked on by a senior girl, so I defended her (as Pam had defended me).

The bully said to me, "If I ever see you outside of school I'm gonna kick your ass!"

"Yeah right, yeah right, yeah right," I kept repeating loudly as she went on and on with her threats.

Once again, it was a big girl. I acted like I wasn't scared, but I was. This one I named Blotch Head. She had this hideous punk hair cut that did her no justice, with blotches of purple like a leopard. Again, I'm not one to make fun of anyone, but when someone was rotten towards me, all I saw was the ugliness in them.

And again, in the midst of the bullying I had an extremely full teenage life. While most girls were dreaming about the prom, I was going to concerts, sneaking into night clubs, meeting rock stars, shopping for clothes in Greenwich Village, and dreaming about writing my first book. I kept diaries and wrote religiously. At parties I mixed in good with other kids.

In one of my classes we had to write an anonymous composition on what we're depressed about. I wrote three brief sentences about how I got depressed coming to "this dump." And that most of the boys and girls were "total fools." It was a little cry for help, but the teacher never confronted me about it. Nevertheless, I was happy with myself for being honest.

Four months before graduation, I got an anonymous phone call in the middle of the night. A female voice threatened, "One step dear, I'm coming near." I thought that was so goofy. I was going to see The Boomtown Rats the next night, and I was thinking maybe someone was going to start with me at the concert. All of a sudden everyone in school was starting to like punk and new wave. Some didn't even like the music but were getting the punk haircuts.

The "trend" I embraced a year ago was now popular. And I honestly believe people resented me for that. Back in those days, you didn't get concert tickets *on line*, you had to wait *in line*. What was once something fun, was now stressful because I'd see the bullies in line for the same concerts I was going to. Whereas a year before a punk or new wave concert was the last place you'd see them!

A friend of mine got bicycle chains for us to carry in our purses to the concert, just in case. Turned out no one bothered me at that concert or any other one.

But every other night or so I'd have a dream about getting into fights with one of the bullies. The dreams were long and vivid. I'd always defend myself in the dreams. What a sad thing to have in your subconscious every night. Sometimes in the dreams, I'd become friends with the bullies. This shows what a good kid I was. Always looking for the best in people.

Then there were the dreams where I ran away from home and lived in Greenwich Village. Those were the kind of dreams I had. I never thought about killing myself as bullied teens do today. During my school years two teenage boys I knew hung themselves in the woods. The first hung himself over a girl. The second, I don't know why.

I knew once school ended there would be a light at the end of the tunnel. With only a few months to go, I got by with average grades during the day. And by night, it was my punk rock world.

The Plasmatics were a very popular punk rock band, unlike any other. Their lead singer Wendy O. Williams trashed Cadillacs onstage, smashed TV sets, and cut guitars with chainsaws. They were at a local record store doing a meet and greet.

Their drummer, Stu Deutsch asked me if I was going to their show that night. I was only 17, and though I had fake I.D. to get into nightclubs, it didn't always work. I told him I was too young. He put me and all my friends on the guest list.

That night, he walked through the crowd to find me and asked if I had any trouble getting in!

In later years I reconnected with Stu. He endorsed my first book, *On the Guest List: Adventures of a Music Journalist*. He also had me, and my husband, at his home. We spent hours talking about The Plasmatics and going through old memorabilia. After *On the Guest List* was published, Stu and I did a meet and greet together at Randy Now's Man Cave in Bordentown, New Jersey. Randy Now was a famous promoter back in the day and now Man Cave is one of the coolest record stores in New Jersey.

Right before summer, I joined up with some younger classmates and we formed a punk rock band called The Defects. I sang and wrote songs. And played a device called a sound gizmo, which hooked up to an amp. It made cool sounds like sirens.

I cut my hair myself, spiking it up and I got compliments from kids in school, not insults. I even overheard my mom telling a friend on the phone how cute I looked. There were some girls that were still disrespectful. They were always so rude to say nasty things loud, so I could hear. As I write this, I realize it was jealousy because in years to come, many of them did the same thing—cut their hair, wear combat boots, and buy a leather jacket. Or they'd keep the same hairstyle they had in high school, well into 2018! Just goes to show that the ones who always made fun of others are the ones who are laughable now.

There's a running joke that most guys don't like women with short hair, but I always found the ones who did. They were the most interesting--either artists, musicians, or just all around cool guys. One who I dated on and off for a few years told me he liked my hair cut spiky. I believe him because he also said that Wendy O. Williams looked better with the mohawk then she did with the long blonde/pink hair. It took many years for the world to catch up to Wendy O. Williams and start sporting fauxhawks. But back in 1981, that haircut was a threat.

Two of the musicians in my band, The Defects, got their hair cut into mohawks. They were brother and sister. Their mohawks shocked people back then. I'll never forget being on line at a White Castle after a concert. A tough woman, probably in her 40s, or even 50s, straight out told the girl, "That's ugly." I felt so bad for her, but I wasn't going to get into it with a woman who looked like she'd carry a knife. This was Passaic, New Jersey. And it was a bad area back in 1981.

How pathetic that a haircut could cause such controversy!

Aside from being criticized for how I chose to wear my hair (and how my friends chose to wear their hair) what really irked me was that people hated music they never even heard. I honestly don't think one kid in my high school heard a punk rock record album.

Boys would see me in the hall and scream, "Punk sucks!" followed by "Devo sucks!" They were too stupid to know that Devo was not a punk rock band. One day it was about 10 boys screaming at me.

I screamed back, "You don't even know what punk is!" And that shut them up.

It happened again in gym class, two guys screamed at me, "Devo sucks." They weren't in my gym class; they were just observing; watching the girls I guess.

I walked right up to them and said, "Do you even know what a real punk rock band is? Have you ever heard of The Dead Kennedys?"

They shook their heads "no."

"Then shut up!" I said.

They didn't know what to say and left me alone. Then, of course, word got out around the high school. By now I was just so nonchalant about people in my school. I was more concerned about music and what concert I was going to next. I said my piece and was done with it.

Now don't get me wrong, it wasn't that I didn't like new wave. I had such eclectic tastes in music, it wasn't just punk rock. I liked punk, new wave, no wave, power pop, rock, and even The Grateful Dead, though I wouldn't admit it to the assholes who bothered me. How hypocritical that The Grateful Dead represented hippies and peace and freedom, yet these kids were anything but peaceful and free.

Another band I really liked was The Bay City Rollers and I got the opportunity to hang out with them when they recorded an album in New Jersey. I spent an evening at the mansion they were living in during that time. A high school girlfriend took me with her. We had so much one on one time chatting with all of them, though it was hard to decipher the Scottish accents.

I really hit it off with the guitarist Eric Faulkner. He zoomed in on me right away because I had on my leather jacket with some buttons. He referred to me as "Punkette." He shared stories that he was friends with Billy Idol. He couldn't remember his name and called him "Blondie." But I realized right away who he meant. Billy Idol was still in Generation X at the time, and not yet the solo sensation he became. He wanted me to go up to his room with him, but I declined. I wasn't interested in a one-night stand with someone I so highly admired.

Every so often I'd go back to Neuman Prep to see a Battle of the Bands. I'd see my old friends; and everyone was so nice. It was like night and day. I'd have so much fun I wouldn't want to leave.

But back at my stupid school it was the same nonsense day in and day out. "Punk sucks! Devo sucks!" I noticed one of the boys saying this had on a Black Sabbath t-shirt. Now, I liked Black Sabbath, so I was familiar with their work.

The next day I was prepared.

There was a section in the hallway that my friends and I called "The Village." We put up a sign that read "The Village" whenever we hung out there in between classes. I came up with a plan. If these dumb kids kept calling Devo "punk" then Black Sabbath, a heavy metal band, was going to be changed to "reggae."

My friends and I took our shoes off and rolled up our pants like we were in the islands. We turned over the garbage cans and played a reggae drum beat on them. I sang the lyrics of "Iron Man" to a reggae beat.

When those boys passed by, they were speechless. After our song I said, "If Devo is punk, then Black Sabbath is reggae."

They never bothered us again.

Near the end of the school year they were sending out ballots. My name was on the ballot for "Most Punk." It was between me and Blotch Head. I wrote in my diary, "I better win." I was truly the more authentic punk, whereas Blotch Head just had purple spots in her hair but wore Grateful Dead shirts and Jesus sandals. She was not punk. Plus, I put up with so much shit, I really felt I earned the title. It was just two months before the end of the year. I started telling some of my friends to vote for me. And I did get the title of "Most Punk" in the yearbook.

Chapter 13

Just one month until graduation and I ended up getting into a fight with Brit again. She started with me again in the gym locker room.

I said something back.

Then she flipped it around and made it seem like I was the one starting trouble. "Don't start with me!" she said as she kicked my sneaker down the aisle.

I threw my other sneaker at her but missed. Then I saw the gym teacher and yelled at her. "You really need to control the locker room!"

The gym teacher set it up so that Brit and I had to go to see the guidance counselor. As I wrote earlier, Brit was a year older than me because she had to stay back a year. So not only was she much bigger than me, she was 18 and picking on a minor.

The next day turned out Brit got away with what she did to me. No detention. Nothing. Schools were so unfair. But let me back up a bit. There was a time I didn't mention. Back when I was still with Aaron, Brit was sitting on the floor in the girl's room, crying.

She noticed me looking at her and said, "At least you have somebody!"

I took this as the opportunity to be friends with her again. I compassionately listened to her babble. I sincerely felt really bad for her. When I brought this up to the guidance counselor, in front of Brit, Brit denied it ever happened.

The guidance counselor insisted our problems were "clash of personality," and "something that started in grade school."

I didn't see it that way. I was willing to be friends. I never understood what happened in grade school. Like I said, the trouble started right after that swimming pool incident. But I can never be positive if that was it.

I will say that this experience prepared me for life in a way. Some people will stop being your friend without explaining why. Even as adults, people do these immature things. The song "People" by Barbra Streisand says it all.

However, I will say that, to me, a good friend is someone who is there; and you can count on. I am not of the mindset that "absence makes the heart grow fonder." I am not one of these people who likes to go for years not talking to someone and then "not missing a beat." I'm an "out of sight, out of mind person." Either you're my friend or you're not. No second guessing. And when I'm friends with someone, they know I love them too. It's a win-win. And if I have something to say, I will say it. I'm not passive-aggressive. I don't like passive-aggressive people.

So, right up to the very end I was having nightmares from time to time about getting beat up. Even though I had at least three cute boys calling me at any given time; and had a very active social life, always going to concerts and NYC with my sister, cousin, and friends. Sometimes the hate really got to me; other times I ignored it. Back then there weren't many all-ages shows and I often got home around 3 a.m. and went to school dead tired and with bruises all over my body from getting knocked around at the general admission shows where you didn't have seats and fought to get upfront. And I was always up front! I also now had a boyfriend in college who had a radio show and worked the door at a night club. He'd often take me out to breakfast around 3 a.m. when he got off either of his shifts. After breakfast we'd sit outside talking and watch it get lighter and lighter out.

Even on so little sleep I really excelled in class, in areas I was interested in like writing. I wrote a Child Rearing Theory and got an A. The teacher praised me in front of the class and I overheard jealous mouths talking about me while the teacher was speaking.

And speaking of jealous mouths, this brings me to rumors. There was a girl who I am still friends with today. We went to concerts together and slept over each other's houses. I even took her along on some of my dates, down the shore, and to New York City. We were developing a great friendship. She was fun, and insightful for a young person. Advice she gave me back then, still holds true today.

I had failed my driver's test about three times. So, some of her friends started a rumor that I was using her for her car. They brainwashed her into believing it enough to confront me about it. I was devastated. I never used anyone in my life and I certainly wasn't using her for her car. My mother brought me almost anywhere I'd want to go. She called herself, "Mom's Taxi Service." I also had an older cousin Jimmy who was really into music. He drove my sister and me to many concerts, also taking this certain friend with us. Plus, as mentioned, I had boyfriends and other friends who drove cars. So how could I be using her for her car when I had so many options? It made no sense. Then, if you really knew my teenage personality, which is also my personality in my 50s, if I like someone, I like them; and if I don't like someone, I don't like them. I don't use people.

    I was mad, and hurt, that she'd even think such a thing. So, I stopped talking to her and was even mean to her if I saw her in the hallway. Eventually we became friends again and all was forgiven on both ends. To this day she is one of my best friends. It just goes to show that the truth always comes out and bad people can't come between good ones.

Chapter 14

Three days before school ended I kept getting anonymous phone calls from someone threatening to beat me up the last day of school. That day I rebelliously wore my Catholic uniform from the Catholic grammar school I went to. That's how thin I was, at age 17, going on 18, it still fit.

With my punk rock friends, we had a little harmless fun. We smashed records and sprayed shaving cream all over the school walls. Nothing that couldn't be fixed; nothing destructive. All innocent. Nevertheless, it was the talk of the school.

No one beat me up either. It was done. Finished. And that was that. To this day I'm so happy I don't have to relive the nightmare again.

I got my diploma but didn't go to the graduation ceremony. I stopped having nightmares about bullies. Now my dreams were about convincing bouncers to let me in clubs to see bands while I was still underage.

Kim got my yearbook for me. She was still a freshman. Since I didn't take school seriously, I didn't take my yearbook seriously either. First, I didn't put my picture in the yearbook. For Ambition I jokingly wrote "Groupie." For Secret Ambition I wrote "Never Mind." After my short and sassy write-up, I ended with, "Blah, blah, blah, and I love you with a knife," taken from the Sex Pistols song, "Great Rock 'n' Roll Swindle."

What happened at my graduation party will stay at my graduation party. It was certainly a wild time. It went on from 1:30 in the afternoon until after midnight. All my punk rock friends were there, each special in their own way. From that moment on, I lived life to the fullest. And I still do.

I DON'T WANT TO BE LIKE YOU

Chapter 15

My mother couldn't afford to send me to college, so I was looking for a job right away. But within days of graduating, there was a magical omen. In my teenage innocence, I wrote a letter to *The Aquarian Arts Weekly*, a music newspaper that had been around since 1969. The published letter went on about how great The Plasmatics are.

Because I didn't have college education, and because I was always the late bloomer, it took some time to figure out what I wanted to do in life. But before my 32nd birthday my articles were being published all over the world. I made a career out of writing, then later editing and ghost writing. I had three books published. Two were self-published; and the last was picked up by a traditional publisher. And of all the books I edited and helped ghost write, as of now, at least 15 are available on Amazon. I also became a public speaker and even spoke at Montville High School, Montville, New Jersey about anti-bullying.

In my first book, *On The Guest List: Adventures of a Music Journalist*, I spoke briefly about being bullied. My homeroom teacher, Michael, wrote me an email after reading the book. He said that if he knew I was bullied he would have kicked some ass. I always acted "cool" in his homeroom. I never played "victim." But I was also embarrassed about being bullied.

This is what I say to kids today who are being bullied. You are not the embarrassment. The bullies are. There is nothing embarrassing about being singled out for being different. But hating someone for being different is shameful and disgusting.

Just keep being yourself. I always say be YOUnique!

A few years ago, I had lunch with a girl who was also bullied in my grade school. She said to me, "Why did they bully us? What did they bring to the table?"

What did they bring to the table? was a good question. Making fun of others certainly isn't something to be proud of. You can do the greatest thing in the world, but if you have hate in your heart, it takes you down several notches.

I don't resent the bullies at all. I do pity them and hope for their sake that they changed for the better. And more important, they aren't raising their kids to be bullies.

Meanwhile, at 55, thanks to my career in writing, I interviewed almost every musician I ever wanted to meet and was on the guest list countless times. Because of my books, I've been on radio shows all over the country. People all over the world read my books. Every day is an adventure and I can honestly say I'm happy most of the time.

I'm happily married and happily without children. I never had the desire for them. Not to say I don't love kids, which is why I'm writing this book. I want every kid out there to know that you can be bullied in school and there can still be a happy-ending. I want the suicide rate of children in school to go down to zero. In a perfect world, all kids would love and accept each other.

I also want to say that bullying doesn't end in school. You don't get bullied at jobs in the traditional way, but bosses can berate you and/or co-workers can be jealous and petty. Sometimes you can make bad choices in the friend or dating pool; or even a bad marriage. But no matter what your situation, there's always a way out and always something good to look forward to in the future. Just keep believing in yourself and don't ever compromise who you are.

From time to time I've struggled with depression and made a choice not to go on medication. I've tried it once and it's not for me. With a holistic mindset, I choose a healthy lifestyle. I eat clean foods, meditate, and practice yoga daily. I surround myself with positive people. I don't gossip; I just say what's on my mind.

In addition to being healthy, one thing I find helpful is to always have something to look forward to. Back in my school days, I'd list upcoming concerts on my school notebooks. To this day, I still do that, but now on my calendar.

When I graduated high school, my sister said the most genius thing, "Now you should wish the time to go very slow."

The time did go slow because I packed so much fun into my 55 years. Some people look back on their lives and ask themselves, "Where did all the time go?"

I know where all my time went because I have diaries from age 15 to current times, filled with all the good times.

And she lived happily ever after; the end!

Special Thanks!

As always to my amazing husband who is my heart and soul, Dennis Mistretta.
To our kitty Nicholas, our little fluff of inspiration.
To our kitties in Heaven, Billy Cat and Derick.
To my Grandma in Heaven, for always being my biggest fan during my humble beginnings.
To God, Jesus Christ, Buddha, angels, fairies, animal spirits, the Universe, Gurdjieff, and other spiritual entities, and masters, for guidance and love along my beautiful path.
To Pop Mistretta in Heaven for always believing in me and saying, "Rome wasn't built in a day."
To Joe Mistretta, for all your loving support!
To my mother, Charlotte Grimes, who loved me and did a great job raising me.
To my zany sister Kim Cagiao, who had her own struggles with bullying and has overcome it, and turned out to be a beautiful, sweet inspiration!
To my nephew Matthew for rocking it!
To Jayne DiGregorio "Michele" for being a super-duper friend, love your "Romy."
To Rebecca Benston, Higher Ground publishing goddess. I am beyond blessed that our paths crossed. Working with you has been absolutely delightful! Thank you for believing in my story!
To the famous promoter Randy Now, of Randy Now's Man Cave, thank you so much for hosting my book signings every year! (And to Margie Anderson, my beautiful, animal-loving friend and "fan" who always shows up to buy my latest book! I'm banging them out for you, hun!)
To Maryann Castello for having me on your fabulous "Health & Wellness" show—which gave me the platform to speak about this book, "I Don't Want to Be Like You" for the very first time on camera!
To Anthony Sia for having me speak about anti-bullying at Montville High School and being a spokesperson for the Coalition for the Human Condition.
And finally, to Pam Macek, for defending me, not once, but twice, to those bullies. You so rock!

I DON'T WANT TO BE LIKE YOU

Maryanne, Grade School

Maryanne, Age 15

Maryanne, Age 16

Maryanne, Age 17

Maryanne, Age 17

Maryanne and husband, Dennis

Other titles from Higher Ground Books & Media:

Wise Up to Rise Up by Rebecca Benston

A Path to Shalom by Steen Burke

From a Hole in My Life to a Life Made Whole by Janet Kay Teresa

Overcomer by Forrest Henslee

Miracles: I Love Them by Forest Godin

32 Days with Christ's Passion by Mark Etter

The Magic Egg by Linda Phillipson

The Tin Can Gang by Chuck David

Whobert the Owl by Mya C. Benston

For His Eyes Only by John Salmon

Out of Darkness by Stephen Bowman

Knowing Affliction and Doing Recovery by John Baldasare

Add these titles to your collection today!

http://highergroundbooksandmedia.com

Made in the USA
Middletown, DE
30 September 2018